Poetics of Soul & Fire

Books by Cheryl Lafferty Eckl

Personal Growth & Transformation

A Beautiful Death:
Keeping the Promise of Love

A Beautiful Grief:
Reflections on Letting Go

The LIGHT Process:
Living on the Razor's Edge of Change

Wise Inner Counselor Books
Reflections on Being Your True Self in Any Situation
Reflections on Doing Your Great Work in Any Occupation
Reflections on Ineffable Love: from loss through grief to joy

Poetry for Inspiration & Beauty

Poetics of Soul & Fire

Bridge to the Otherworld

Idylls from the Garden of Spiritual Delights & Healing

Sparks of Celtic Mystery:
soul poems from Éire

A Beautiful Joy: Reunion with the Beloved
Through Transfiguring Love

Twin Flames Romance Novels

The Weaving:
A Novel of Twin Flames Through Time

Twin Flames of Éire Trilogy
The Ancients and The Call
The Water and The Flame
The Mystics and The Mystery

Poetics of Soul & Fire

Cheryl Lafferty Eckl

FLYING CRANE PRESS

*For those who
dare to dance
between the here & there.*

POETICS OF SOUL & FIRE
© 2015, 2021, 2022 by Cheryl J. Eckl, LLC

Published by Flying Crane Press, Livingston, Montana 59047
Cheryl@CherylEckl.com | www.CherylEckl.com

All rights reserved. No part of this book may be used, reproduced, translated, electronically stored, or transmitted in any manner whatsoever without prior written permission from the author or publisher, except by reviewers, who may quote brief text-only passages in their reviews.

Library of Congress Control Number: 2015913536
ISBN: 978-0-9828107-8-1 (paperback)
ISBN: 978-0-9828107-9-8 (e-book)

Printed in the United States of America

*When life is an adventure
and Spirit the guide,
anything can happen—
and usually does.*

The Seer of Soul & Fire

Gazing into crystal, she muses.

Worlds and wonders swim before her.

Death resting on the table at her side—
    the inevitable presence that reveals
    life's worth and meaning.

Eternity stirs anew in the orb.

Beckoning from the Unknown, she feels it—
    a future from the past,
    a glimmering sense of purpose,
    a dream of communion with the Beloved—
        the found that was lost,
        and yet, the One still truly here.

Destiny proclaims its work in the glass—
    oneness forever sealed
    in the heart of her ancient calling.

Contents

The Seer of Soul & Fire vi

Worlds & Wonders
    Childhood Intimations 3
    Goddess Rising 4
    Heart Murmurs 7
    The Turning Point—A Dialogue 8
    Initiate's Chamber 12
    A Vision 14
    The Liminal 15
    Celtic Dreams 16
    The Magus 18

Beckoning from the Unknown
    Dreamer's Guide 23
    Fire Ceremony 24
    Resistance 26
    Dark Water 27
    The Net 28
    The Fortune Teller 29
    The Wild 32
    The Panther 33
    Voice in the Tunnel 34
    Shaman Call 36
    Save Your Child 38
    The Soul That's Never Been Lost 40

A Dream of Communion

Why Love 45
Time Will Tell 46
Missed Connection 48
Asking for Help 49
Thawing 50
Compatriot 52
Mirroring 53
The Conversation 54
Simply Loving 55
Visitation from the Man in White 56
Trust 58
The Wedding 59
Soliloquy 60
Thinning of the Veil 61
For My Friend, the Rower 62
Invisible to Me 63
Prayer for a Soul Friend 64

The One Still Truly Here

Letting Go 69
Gratitude's Elixir 70
Breaking Through 72
Letting a Hard Day Be 73
The Lament 74
What Wizards Know 76
Puzzling 77
Paso Doble—Spirals in the Dark 78

Grace 80
Mother's Day 81
In Her Shoes 82
Making My Own Tracks 84
A Vision of Passages 85
Thoughts at Midnight 86
Dawn's Song 87
Past as Prologue 88
Quantum Leaping 89
An Open Vessel 90

Destiny Proclaims

Thoughts Upon Embarking 95
Finding Gold in the Interval 96
Intimations of the Future 98
Unpredictable 99
The Shift 100
Navigating the Doldrums 102
Attunement 104
The Catalyst 105
What If? 108
At Day's End 110
A Glimmering Sense of Purpose 111

ILLUSTRATIONS

Crystal Ball, John William Waterhouse, 1902 vii

Windflowers, John William Waterhouse, 1902 xii

The Bells, Edmund Dulac, 1912 20

The Knave of Hearts Watching Lady Violette Depart,
Maxfield Parrish, 1925 42

The Soul of the Rose, John William Waterhouse, 1908 . . . 66

Destiny, John William Waterhouse, 1900 92

*One need not travel
across the sea
to abide for a while
between worlds.*

Childhood Intimations

Sitting in my apple tree
as high as I could safely climb,
leafy branches cradled me
as devas spoke in whispered tones
of mysteries and magic tales,
of star-lit homes and secret worlds
where children laugh to see themselves
as crystal beams of sparkling light—
much less as bodies than as souls.

Most of what they said is lost,
except the knowing in my bones
that I could visit them at will
(even when my tree was gone)
to step between the veil of time—
and words would always take me there.

Goddess Rising

Through gauzy mists of memory she comes.
Faintly at first, no more than whispered breath,
She beckons, then withdraws.

There is no sound,
But only hush of flowing robes and lisping trees
That give away her passing—but not quite.

She lingers just outside of thought
And intimates her presence in my mind.
I feel her watching as I peer into the past.
    O, I was there! And she.

We walked as one and were.
Though I had run away in fear
She yet remained and waited—
    Waited, waited

Not stepping through the mist
Till I stepped first.

I see me now, midst tree-lined vales
And circles in the dark.

The moon is out and that is all I see
As if a single window clears
And then clouds shut.

It is enough to feel, to feel—
    O, I was there!

A priestess Celt, a Druidess perhaps,
On ancient Éire.

A leader—one who knew the sacred truths
At least as Truth was known in nature and in art.
    I knew! I knew!

And carried in myself a threat to those
Who changed our ways
For nothing more than lust and greed.

I do not see the end—the glass is dark
And yet I know it.
    Aye.

The tortured pain.
The shattered disbelief in life.
And then the lie:

It is not safe to be myself.
To utter what I am.
To heal.
To practice in the glen or sing or dance
Or show myself a priestess come again.

Her time appears—and mine,
That none may stop;
For now I see behind the lie.
Too dangerous to be?
    Not so!

How many years and lifetimes past and gone?
        Or none…

The truth slips in and heals,
Lifting the shroud of darkness
As she blends into my mind and heart
And I look out upon the world
As with new eyes—yet old.

My eyes and hers—the same,
Infused with power
And with joy to know and be
She that I bore and barred for fear—till now
        Till now, till now.

I feel her wisdom rise and I am free.

Heart Murmurs

Spirit flows where it wishes
and the heart hums along.

You need not know what is arising—
only that life will never be the same.

Drop down where Mystery dwells,
to your soul's secret home—
that full, quiet place of deep communion
where only gentle feet may enter in.

Change is different here
in the brilliant caverns of true being—
where Light dispels bleak darkness
because Divinity has revealed
your innermost reality.

Hummmmm....

The Turning Point—A Dialogue

The Master

>Walk the circle, my beloved,
>In the ritual of the hours,
>Climb the pathway, scale the mountains.
>Be the hero in the labyrinth.
>Slay the Minotaur that binds you.
>Walk the circle in my footsteps.

The Disciple

>Lead, O Bright One, I will follow.
>I have seen you on the mountain
>Draw the fiery ring from heaven,
>Cast to earth the blazing circlet
>To consume the maudlin woes there.
>Lead me onward in your power.

The Master

>Walk the circle of my wisdom,
>Inward, outward, forward, backward.
>Time becomes as weaving garments,
>Yet of light, not earthly matter.
>They will clothe you, if you faint not.
>Are you ready for your testing?

The Disciple

>I am bold and brave—a warrior.
>My accomplishments are mighty.
>*Shining One* and *Fair* they call me.
>I am worthy, yes, and ready.
>I will fail not in this challenge.

The Master
> Walk the circle, my beloved.
> Eat the bread of my salvation.
> Take the cup of life and loving.
> It will taste both sweet and bitter,
> Yet is proof of my forewarnings.
> Haste not to the fray unarmored.

The Disciple
> I fear not, Adoring Master,
> You so wise in sweet compassion.
> Only fools would miss the victory
> While enfolded in such beauty.
> But for Love I will obey you.
> Eager am I for the challenge.

The Master
> 'Round 'n 'round the cycles spinning.
> Not one circle, but a dozen,
> Moving as you walk upon them.
> Past is present, future past here.
> You must run, lest time o'ertake you.
> Faster! I would see you conquer!

The Disciple
> Master, Bright One! Help me! Save me!
> I am sinking in the quagmire.
> Darker circles lie in wait here—
> Hollow horrors, night and blackness.
> I misunderstood your warnings.
> I saw not. O, I am dying.

The Master
> I had hoped you'd heed my warning.
> These are circles of your making.
> Light and dark are both your castings
> On the waters of your pathway.
> O, despair not, Tender-hearted;
> I will lend my hand to guide you.

The Disciple
> Thank you, Master, for your kindness.
> I am brave, a steadfast fighter.
> I can stand to face the giant.
> All your teachings are the signposts,
> Not so hard to follow homeward.
> You have laid a clear course, Master.

The Master
> Pass the test, then, if you will to.
> Do you challenge light or darkness?
> By whose power will you conquer?
> Walk the circle in the shadow
> Of your deeds, both ill and noble.
> Walk the circle of your choosing.

The Disciple
> Bravery stand, O courage, faint not!
> Heart expand, the beast looms frightening.
> Why is darkness all around me?
> Where is light to see the circle?
> Where is help? I fight alone now.
> Master, save me! Strike a torch here!

The Master
> Angels, tend the bleeding warrior.
> In his hand a sword of light place.
> Bind the dragon in his lair.
> Lead the fair one to his victory.
> Will he hear your garments rustling?
> Does he know who won the skirmish?

The Disciple
> Father, Bright One, stretch your hand forth.
> Heal my bruised and battered body.
> Yours the power; yours the glory.
> I was lost, had you not answered.
> You are Master of the Circle.
> I am weary—kneel before you.

The Master
> Rise up, Son of Light, in victory.
> You have won a mighty battle.
> See the carcass there before you.
> 'Tis the beast of your own slaying.
> You have conquered by your heart's will.
> And the power of Love between us.

The Disciple
> I accept your approbation.
> Yet I lay it on the altar.
> By your grace I vanquished darkness.
> Only Love has brought me homeward.

The Master
> Walk the circle now in oneness.
> I am at your side, Beloved.

Initiate's Chamber

The desert shimmers in Giza's mesmerizing heat
        as a silent caravan glides
        across the blistering sands,
        greeting no one and warning curious eyes
        to avert their gaze.

Here is no idle crossing but a ritual act,
        an initiation
        known only to the few
        who dare to face the ultimate step.

Mysteries long forgotten will be awakened tonight
        by one whose time has come
        to descend the secret stairway,
        to seek answer to life's great questions.

The unenlightened believe
        a tomb filled with riches lies here;
        so it does—
        but only the ego dies in this place,
        and the riches are not of this world,
        but of the soul.

For this descent is to the heart of being itself—
        a perilous journey from which
        some do not return.

Perhaps gone mad or dumbstruck,
        they do not emerge whole—
        such is the eventual test
        for those who would be free,
        and yet live to serve again.

The patterns of fear must dissolve
        so that Love may live
        and the soul thrive in a reality
        that sets all thoughts aright.

Is it any wonder that we tremble
        when the door swings open?

I am handed a torch and bade to step in
        as the portal closes silently behind me.

A Vision

Far off the southern coast of Italy
Lies a tiny, mythic island—
Basking in the Mediterranean sun,
Glistening with a secret radiance
One only sees clearly by moonlight.

An enigmatic man reclines there,
Neither eager nor expectant—
Content to navigate the threshold
Where sand and sea and sky
Hold their deepest conversations.

The air hangs thick with promise here.
Yet only mystics part the veil
Twixt Rome and Arabi,
And daily make the choice
To turn upon division and
Walk out on the waters
Of Spirit's other world.

The Liminal

Surely I am she who disappears
    behind the screen
    to change her garments
    into something more invisible.

Not to show a body,
But to illuminate its absence—
To call upon the soul that wants to appear,
    yet knows the danger
    of being too much in the world.

These are secret rites.
The transformation into gossamer
Is for the few who tread lightly upon earth
    and dare to dance
    between the here and there.

Today is disappearing into dark
    while a new sun slumbers
    'neath an unknown horizon.

Transition is too big for words,
Too faint, except to feel its coming
And to know one's self in its alignment.

Such is the life of the liminal ones
Who slip beneath the waves of change,
Only to reappear upon the beach—
    all dry and fresh,
    wearing new wings,
    and looking at the sun.

Celtic Dreams

Bards of old sang soulfully
    of rocks and rivers,
    lakes and mountains
    sublime in their antiquity;

    with fields aflame in wildflowers,
    bending breezily in full knowing
    that vibrant life for them is short,
    yet powerful in its glory.

At peace upon yon dream-like hillside
    a mystic troubadour
    appears to wander,
    his lungs filled up
    with clover's heady sweetness,

    his eyes affixed on a cloudless ceiling,
    his ears attuned to subtle sounds
    of insect creatures skittering
    in tall grass,

    and all the portals of his mind
    unfettered by such worldly thoughts
    as have no place
    in nature's great cathedral.

He stays awhile, then drifts away.
    (Éire's minstrel belongs to dreamtime.)
    And as he fades my mind inquires—

Could I but sound reality's tone
    that hums the deep bass
    of Terra's grounded presence,
    and beckons my heart
    to loftier climes,

    where Spirit's voice speaks clearly
    as a sunbeam's noontime filament,

    then, surely, in that fair place
    mystery's song would
    awaken my soul
    and life's full joy be mine at last—
        all the way to forever.

The Magus

Standing in his wisdom grove,
Back turned, sensing my approach,
He feels a smile form on his lips,
Then tucks it away to greet me—
And so you've come.

Yes, is all I say.
I've learned not to blather,
Even as my heart races
And I long to run to his embrace.
To be acknowledged and truly seen
Suffices at this moment.

Come, he beckons,
Descending mossy steps
To the spring-fed well he tends.

Drink, he motions,
As I kneel beside crystal waters
And lift the clear elixir to my lips.

This is the moment of acceptance,
When past and present-future all converge
In a single realization
      of identity and promise,
      of prelude and obligation,
      of possibility and discernment.

I will, is my reply to his unspoken inquiry—
The only true response of student to Teacher,
The matter of choice,
> spoken from the razor's edge
> where all is lost or won,
> where victory and defeat
> are sistered in appearance
> until their shawls come off.

I will, he answers my heart's plea,
Placing ancient hands of holy water
On my brow and whispering my new name.

Now go and come back when I call you.
You will know what to do,
> and where and when,
> with the blessing of hospitality
> as your surety and guide.

Feel it in your heart and follow where it leads.
Stoke the inner fires and do the radical thing.
I will be there in the water and the flame
As I have always, ever been.

Beckoning from the Unknown

*Only egos go to sea in destroyers.
For waters wild and deep,
souls navigate in tall ships with love
and a zest for stormy weather.*

The Dreamer's Guide

I am she who dips into water
        to ripple the surface
        and lure deep thoughts
        up from their hiding place
        'neath waves of feeling
        long rejected or forgot.

You know the sea holds secrets
        that you cringe to view;
        but unlocked they must be,
        for only in damp darkness
        is the answer to be found.

Dry land is not your native home—
        never mind familiar comfort
        that you've found
        upon the margins.

Follow me from shore to shoal.

You will not drown in my company,
        though we plunge
        to murky passages
        of weakness and past fear.

Give me your hand
        and we'll bring up pearls
        from beds long-cleansed of relics.

My likeness holds no monsters.

Fire Ceremony

Meet me in the Otherworld, he said,
      and I will show you
      what it's like
      to rest in Light.

There's something
      that you need to know
      about the past that blocks—

An ancient fear of dreams
      you've spent your
      whole life running from.

Sit still, my darling, by water's edge,
      and do not resist
      Love's mysteries
      that call you forth.

You have the power
      at your fingertips,
      the wisdom
      in your garments.

The underground seed
      is nearly set to bloom,
      but the old ways must go.

You are so much more
      than anyone's opinion.

Die the good death
>> to all that is false,
>> >> and be transition's offspring.

A fire is coming,
>> and it will shake you
>> to your core.

The Phoenix bird is rising.

Resistance

At last she saw the impediment—
    like a barricade, an armed camp,
    circled 'round with a moat
    and a drawbridge—
        a castle keep to protect
        the princess.

But facing out, she missed the threat
    that sifted in like smoke
    under the door,
    poisoning the air, the food,
    filling her with a different fear,

    not trusting those who fed her,
    resisting what would save her,
    locking herself up tight
        in a prison to which
        only she had the key.

Allowing the defenses to drop
    and the healers to enter
        will be her biggest battle.

Withdrawing her gaze
    from the outward scene,
        she turned herself around
        and felt an inner door unlock.

Dark Water

The unconscious one lies in wait—
    devourer of children
    murderer of men
    keeper of secrets
    dispeller of lies—
    but only when she wishes to tell the truth.

Meantime, she broods in her aquatic cave,
    reached only by facile swimmers
    who know how to breathe under water.

Dive down!
For you must meet her in her lair—
    the place of overwhelm and lost souls,
    where death and murky light abide,
    and phoenix fire goes out—
    extinguished by her liquid love
    that strangles heroes as they doze.

Dive down!
For only in her dreamland
    do sleepers revive,
    and surge to the surface,
    carrying secrets in their wake,
    and salvation for the drowning.

Have courage!
You do not swim alone here—
    where light meets dark,
    where known meets unknown,
    and the soul comes alive with possibility.

The Net

Were the consequences so dire
Of one false crossing
On board a ship
Across black water
Cold and dark—
So frightfully alone, that now you falter?

Freedom lies across the gap—
A mediocre safety on this side.
Will you dare to jump
And risk the drop?

The prize you seek awaits,
But you can never walk around.
The only way is there—
Across the gap.

What if your fear is nothing—
A mirage, an illusion?
An abyss made of dreams and rumors?
Another lie to be dispelled?

Let go the edges.
Have faith, for once.
You've never seen the net
That's been there all along.

You are the net yourself.
Step out.

The Fortune Teller

Give me yer palm, the gypsy said,
An' I'll tell ye when ye're wealthy or dead.
The hopes an' dreams of yer feminine heart
Are fantasies spun outta angels' art.

O, ye're a shy one, snatch yer hand back!
Ha! Ye'll know anyway, curious cat.
Wouldn't ye see what the future brings?
Captains, traitors, lovers, kings?

See how she pauses an' wonders a-spell.
Don't ye believe? I may not tell ye that
Stories are hidden b'hind yer eyes
That show me ye're relivin' many lives.

Courtesan, sister, beggar, or queen—
All these fine ladies ye have been.
Who will ye be t'day, m'dear?
Find an identity, I don't care.

Spin a reality, gossamer fine.
Weave a new garment—ye're still mine.
I own yer heart—to me ye're still true.
I hold the key to the findin' of you.

Give me yer palm an' I'll show ye the mark
Where we took out the light an' put in the spark
Of darkness, desire—the essence of he
Who manages all of us, includin' thee.

Ha! Are ye shock'd to find us livin'
In yer soul? To us ye're givin'
Substance an' life. Nay, don't go away.
Ye're here till I order ye need not stay.

O, shout if ye want—ye shan't be free.
The spell is unbroken fer centuries.
Ye've done as we lik'd, an' performed well.
Ye've liv'd with a lust come straight from hell.

O, cry to yer savior. He won't hear.
Ye've done it fer eons, an' we're still here.
I mock yer religion—all lies, all sham!
O, cry out! Ye're hopeless!

Indeed? I AM!

What! Don't say those words!
Ye're breakin' the spell!
My handiwork—fragments!
My body—a shell!

That light!
Stop increasin'!
It's growin' to flame.
Get back, wretched creature!
Stop callin' that name!

Give me yer palm! My mark isn't there!
Ye trick'd me! Ye're an angel!
Ye came from the air!

Ye're free now. Don't hurt me!
She's singin' a song!
I'm burnin'! Like vapor—
My power is gone......

The Wild

I knew her once—
    The Wild.

The one who lived free
    in exuberant joy,
    in love with being here.

Fearless, sunny—
    a light that shone
    on all she met
    and welcomed
    what might come.

What must fall away
    to get her back?

Only blinders, perhaps,
    or doubt—
    more likely lack of trust
    in her reality.

She was never really far away,
    needing only
    a gentle invitation
    to reappear.

The Panther

I saw the story on Facebook—
A black panther named Diablo
Who had been rescued from abuse,
But who didn't know how to be free
Until the animal whisperer came
And listened to his complaint.

The reason he snarled at everyone,
Refusing to leave his night shelter,
Was because he thought he was
Still expected to perform.

Trusting no one else, he began to relax
When she convinced him
That nothing was demanded of him.

He hated his name—the devil.
So instead they called him Spirit
And simply let him be.

I get it.
And I'd like to be called Alana.

Voice in the Tunnel

You were not assured of hearing me in this life—
    but your childhood yearning was so great,
    your focus so determined,
    that a remnant of our
    ancient contact surfaced;
        and I came forth
        to greet you as of old.

Revealer of Secrets they once called you,
    so intense was your desire
    to plumb the deeper mysteries—
        not for yourself alone
        but for the lost and lonely ones
        who knew not how to seek.

So, as an earnest child, you were allowed
    to hear my voice,
    to view life's gateway
    in a vision of spiral heavens,
    that you might be inspired
    to discover clues and insights
    into some of life's great questions
        that you gradually neglected
        in favor of life's trinkets,
        until your grown-up longing
        bade me break the silence
        once again.

At life's crossroads or its threshold
souls may witness
their own bright tunnel.

There I am
and there I speak,
yet often in tones so faint
that only children
can hear them.

And always, for some,
my voice comes through
in startling clarity—

Much like today,
and the day you still recall,
when your heart's deep need
elicited my emergence,
and veils were lifted for a time
to show you life's source
as its ultimate goal

and to assure you
that Light will lead to Light
if you but follow all the way
to greet the Masters
in their home.

Shaman Call

The powerful Mother beckons again,
    and this time one bright soul must answer,
    for initiation's moment has come
    into mysteries long feared and resisted
    since all went wrong, because of him—
    or so he'd believed for centuries.

He'd been a dreamer once—
    a destined leader of his people,
    a seer who could not stop
    the calamity that had come to pass.

He'd suffered sorely with the others,
    perhaps more so, for he had seen
    and done his best to warn them all—
    if only they had listened.

Dreams move on like rivers,
    and only those we lean into
    can release their power
    to save or salve the nations.

He knows this now,
    and begs to reawaken powers
    long hidden in the depths
    of his past's dark cauldron
    of memories, regrets, and fears.

For the soul, once scarred
    (or twice or thrice),
    reluctantly takes up the orb
    where Truth abides
    and reckons to be spoken.

Such are the trials the Mother brings—
    realistic towards resistance,
    her visage frightening at first,
    then followed by high-flying banners
    that declare in solace
    to the leader come again:

    This time you will not fail, my love!
        Follow me now
        and dance on waves
        of future inspiration!

Save Your Child

He felt like one of those kids
    who'd been conceived
    to save the life of a sibling
    that needs a kidney or a
    bone marrow transplant—
    except he'd come
    to save his mother.

Life wasn't working out
    the way she'd hoped
    so she became obsessed
    with the idea that
    having a baby
    would make her happy.

And the little boy shared her belief.

He was raised on it—
    drank it in as mother's milk;
    the perfect little liberator
    come to earth to free
    a woman from her melancholy.

A child should not be
    made responsible for a parent's
    sense of well-being;
    but that's what happened.

He saw it all so clearly now.

Pondering this sudden revelation,
    while walking down a hallway
    in the home that he had built,
    he caught sight of
    his grown-up image
    in the mirror.

Startled, he paused—
    then moved on
    in self-forgiveness
    midst a blessed realization:

The little boy had been effect,
    not cause,
    and he no longer
    was that child.

Opening the front door,
    he crossed the threshold
    into daylight,
    walked down the street,
    turned a corner,
    and decided to save himself.

The Soul That's Never Been Lost

Once upon a time I was born—again.
Timeless in the midst of a life well chosen.

> *Are you sure?* they had asked.
> This is going to be rough.
> You'll think you're lost.
>
> You'll doubt the love that's
> All around, yet feels distant.
> You'll wonder what happened
> And why you can't find home.
>
> Are you sure you're ready?

I am! I said with determined purpose.
This is my chance and I claim it.

> *So be it,* said the Great One.
> And for your courage, here's the boon—
>
> One day you will discover
> That who you are today,
> How you know yourself to be,
> Will never be lost.
>
> Look into my eyes
> And feel the truth of what I say.
> Remember me, and you will
> Remember yourself forever.

There is no time, no loss,
No unreality in your heart—
Be you child or aged self.

Venture all the way into the picture.
You will find the wise babe
And Love will be your all.

Essence abides.
Have faith in that.

*You are friends of long ago—
dedicated to raising each other up,
equally yoked and equally intent
on vibrant, loving living.*

Why Love?

I do not need you, O, my love,
to satisfy my longing for the things of Spirit;
    for the Divine has filled my heart and mind
    with its fire of tender holiness.

I do not need you by my side
to point the way or show the path of angel feet;
    for angels speak to me as well in clarion tones
    that ring the knell of darkness late.

I do not need you as I go from place to place
while greeting friends who have grown dear;
    for there are parts of me long hid, except
    a certain friend should cross my path and talk.

But, O, I need to love you, my sweet love,
to satisfy my longing for just you;
    for you are simply one with whom
    I am much more than merely me.

With you I am my Self.

Time Will Tell

In truth, dear friend,
I am too fond
and think too often
of the sudden laugh,
the carefree whistle
you send forth
to greet the workday bustle.

You buoy me up, that's sure,
and by your winsome grin
erase a thousand woes
that would tear me
from my purpose
and my joy.

In you, my friend,
I see the softer side of me
that hardly peeps her head
above the surface
of most days
for fear that others
might not be
so kind as you.

And yet the awakening
of this gentle self
brings trembling
to my soul
and makes me wonder:

Should I trust you
with my secrets?

Would you hurt me
like some others?

Or would you be my champion
in the days
and nights to come?

Time will tell,
though time is not yet
telling of the light or sorrow
it may bring.

Meanwhile,
work is helpful
to the unquiet,
wishing mind.

Missed Connection

She found it amazing that one so perfect
    would come to be the one denied;
    but sometimes that's what happens
    when promise fails to equal action.

The one who would have loved him
    reluctantly admitted that
    his was a coward's way—
    to awaken her affection
    with no intent to love.

He had dealt her a cruelty, yet a blessing—
    for decisions are sometimes
    more easily made
    in light of heartaches
    and vivid disappointments.

Connection is sublime and recognition a gift;
    but desiring to be seen,
    we risk too much
    by telling all our secrets.

Such is the path of Truth.

The road to wholeness
    is neither smooth nor straight;
    and highwaymen come riding
    in the garb of friendly pilgrims.

Beware of those who cannot tell
themselves from their disguises.

Asking for Help

Making a mild request
was the best that she could do—
to ask for a few things from the store:
a jug or two of water,
perhaps some ripe bananas.

Such an appeal might have been the moon—
so difficult was accepting aid
from those who love her,
yet whose offers she was wont to refuse.

Admitting to her human frailty
was like rending the temple veil,
so astonishing was her experience
of being in need and realizing
that her needs would be gladly met.

A balm to her soul—
that's how it felt
to receive and to discover
that true friendship flourishes
when others are allowed to help you.

Thawing

Frozen in her world of grief,
She rested in a silent cube of tears,
Grown solid in the dark reflection
That resisted news of brighter climes,
Despite her longing for release.

Forgotten were the days of sun and laughter
When life was green
And roses blossomed in their beds.
That light went out so long ago
It flickered now but dimly in her mind,
Her body cold to those
Who might desire to move her.

And yet she lived in hope of some redeemer
Who might emerge from out the wasteland
Waving a bright banner
And carrying a single red coal
To spark the flame of her revival.

Years ago, the seers had told of such a one
And bade her gaze with care beyond the pale.
The prophecy was enough to make her curious,
Though sans belief, grey-eyed, and
Scanning in the wrong direction.

For the answer would not come
As strangers do—

But as an unwrapped birthday gift,
Left by one of her acquaintance,
A man long-cloaked in obscurity,
Who carried in his mantle a secret fire.

It was weeks before she noticed
A fresh breeze blowing in her hair,
An openness of mind and heart,
Her body oddly talkative,
And all around her pools of salty water.

Compatriot

You marvel that I do not fear you.
How could I?
When we two see eye to eye,
Reflecting back each one's finer self
That rises to the conversation,
Delighting to be seen.

A gift of friendship unlike all others,
Poised for a time between worlds,
Calling our souls to higher purpose,
And showering both with pearls
Of inspiration and resolve.

To be more than one's daily self
Is an act of invisible courage,
Noticed only by those who
Walk the same Camino.

We are dwellers on two planets,
And no one is the wiser
Except we two, whose silent ships
Sail joyfully amongst the stars.

Mirroring

Simpatico, you say.
We are each other's reflection.
    With you as mirror
    my brilliance shines through,
    catching me by surprise
        as it travels down the centuries
        to a point of pure beginning.

Simpatico, I agree.
Projecting your image onto the screen
of my heart, you are illumined.
        Darkness flees as you stand truly,
        basking in your own heart's glow,
            seeing new facets
            of the divine pattern
            that you are.

This is magic of another world—
The one we cannot live in,
    the home we long for,
    the depth of being
    we had not seen so clearly,
        before falling into the mirror
        held up by the other.

The Conversation

The realization came upon her softly—
Noticing how deeply satisfying
It is to talk to a friend
Who gets her, appreciates her.

To feel seen is the greatest blessing.

He likes to talk to her,
And he listens with presence
As well as attunement—

Her colleague/brother
Who would not be a lover,
Yet who clearly loves her soul
And values their connection.

This is a joyful gift—
The receipt of which
Makes her really happy.

Simply Loving

This morning I wondered:
    Is it possible to love everything
        that arises in my life
        or everyone who crosses my path?

    What if, for every hurt, or disagreement,
        slight, disturbance, inconvenience,
        agitation, or complaint
        I could pour love into that wound?

    Would my contribution matter?
        Do small deeds accumulate?
        Are fools the only ones who think so?

But then, this afternoon
    My friend's black lab arrived for a sleepover
        while her master is away—
        and my perspective changed.

    Dog's don't worry about pouring love
        into wounded places.
    They just lick your face,
        smile trustingly into your eyes,
        and climb up next to you
        to snuggle on your sofa
            in the total contentment
            that comes
            from simply loving.

Visitation from the Man in White

Suddenly he appears in my mind's eye,
Clothed in plain white shirt and jeans,
No glasses, trim and straight,
Radiant, but not showy—
Just like himself.

He says nothing.
This is a test to see if I can abide
In this space of his being
Without ripples or concern,
Noticing, accepting, sensing—
Content to listen to what silence conveys.

Did not our hearts burn?
This is proof of presence and communion,
Of possibility and necessity,
Of secrets I am meant to learn,
And a future surpassing all illusions.

I think I hear him speak at last—

> Come with me, follow me,
> I have so much to show you.
> Libraries of ancient wisdom
> That would dwarf Alexandria.
> Laboratories, mathematics,
> Star gazing, geometrizing,
> Opening out upon the Himalayan meadow,
> Iridescent green against azure skies
> And snow-capped peaks.

This is our heaven.
We sit and talk. Or he talks.
I must get used to him free of persona
And let go my own defensiveness
Against projections that are no longer there.

I'm sorry.
We say it together,
Even as we acknowledge what we did right.

I know this man so well;
And yet he remains a mystery.
There are things he cannot tell me
And things he can that I must earn.

Such merit comes from learning
Through rest and meditation,
Drinking in sweet Spirit's essence
And opening my heart to joy
That comes from our communion.

Poetry is still our favored way.
Wordsworth and Browning,
Together as they never were,
Now letting the words flow
Like Rumi, Rilke, and Tagore.

The poems speak for themselves.

Trust

We've been doing this all along—
You and I together,
Partners on the path,
Deeply connected,
Facing the world,
Hand in hand—
And yet, not quite.

For until that clasp is truly felt
And seen with a single eye,
It is not real.

No one is to blame.
There is no shame
In being human—and blind.
That's part of the deal.

But the illusion has been lifted,
The deepest lies exposed.
So now you can trust me
To be here—fully present;
And I can trust you
To tell me when I'm not.

The Wedding

I've come back, he said,
    in order that we may be truly wed.

You were not ready, nor was I;
    for we have seen each other,
    and yet we were not truly known.

There were lessons to learn,
    separation to grieve,
    shared tasks,
    practiced correspondence,
    breaking, emptying, healing,
    and oneness to discover—
    not with each other
    but each one with the Self.

Purgation has been called a holy place
    where letting go is not torment,
    though stretching on the rack
    of growth can feel that way.

In partnership with our finer natures,
    and flexibility of mind and heart
    do we enter at last the bridal chamber.

Kneel with me, my darling,
    that our path may be blessed;
    for we have found each other
    in what Eternity would join for good.

Soliloquy

What was I saying to myself?

Not even a whisper
    is left of what
    once went unsaid.

Gone back to the ethers,
    my thought lost its way
    in the dark
    and doesn't know
    the gate has been left open.

This silent hall
    is not the place
    to encourage
    inspiration's return.

Some pumps need priming,
    and even a too-full well
    needs a bucket to
    haul up the water.

This self requires another self
    with whom to speak
    and discover her unspoken truth.

Thinning of the Veil

Step into my heart, Beloved,
and I will tell you tales
of joy and light and
stars beyond number.

I have been to galaxies
light-years from here,
even as I am anchored to you
over the tie that binds us.

The threshold between worlds
thins here in your sanctuary
and I come closer
as you pray.

Hearts in love create a portal;
your devotion is the key.

Bhakti gives birth to shakti;
that's the secret
of our connection.

For My Friend, the Rower

Reading your poems for the departed
    in a still house
    with tears in my eyes
    and a lump in my throat,
Your words move me to the core.

I now see why we connected
    in friendship at first sight.

Seared to the bone by Death—
    the force that
    takes away bodies
    and liberates essence,
We are joined at the heart.

Mutual courage is what I recognized
    in those early conversations.

How fortunate
    on the path of Selfhood
    to have found a friend
    who faces challenges head-on,
Even when she's rowing backwards.

Invisible to Me

You can't see me, but I'm here,
Just to encourage and support,
With always a discreet distance,
Because this journey is yours to learn
And earn victoriously.

Your destiny is invisible to me.
We're both walking by faith
Through a different kind of separation;
Not between worlds, but between phases.
The future must be lived to be known.

Prayer for a Soul Friend

Anam Cara—that's how the Celts called
    the friend who will see you naked,
    unblemished by the world
    or your own misconceptions.

We humans suffer from mistaken identity—
    assuming ourselves to be other than
    the brilliant soul created by Love
    and acting as unworthily as we
    believe ourselves to be.

Soul friends know otherwise—
    and slip into our lives
    to push, prod, humor, and cajole us
    to look into their eyes and see
    the image of our loveliness
    mirrored back in purity's reflection.

This is gnosis—unschooled knowing—
    recognition deep and sudden
    that, at its core, bears no conditions,
    urging only courage, kindness, and
    attunement with each soul's pledge
    to higher purpose.

All we really have in this life is time;
    and no one has tapped clear prophecy
    to give us the measure of that interval.

Such is the way of *anam cara* that
    cycles may be fleeting and
    lessons more than we can bear—
    or so we think.

But soul friends know that time
    is naught when put to use
    in loving our togetherness and
    cherishing the ties that bind us
    heart to heart—no matter what.

Our beloveds may lift off this plane,
    leaving us to mourn their flight;
    but gentle ears detect a whisper,
    reassuring those who grieve
    that lovers once may be lovers again.

For Love awakened cannot help but find itself
    renewed and recreated
    in life's sweet gift of a new companion
    who comes to share the path we choose
    to journey home together.

Who would not pray for such a partner—
    if even for a little while?

The One Still Truly Here

*Dark fruit is falling from the tree,
and tangled vines of shadow melt away
beneath the gaze of Truth
that shines out from the being
that I am.*

Letting Go

Can I move through the wilderness
    without my stories of the past?

With nothing but an empty notebook,
    a pencil,
    and my felt sense of
    connection beyond the seen?

To journey by the name of traveler
    as an open door
    or a clear pane of glass—

No expectations, no obstacles,
    merely hospitable toward
    the day, the wind, the rain—

Cloaked only in the belief
    that all is for
    my highest good.

Gratitude's Elixir

Loving the lovable is easy—
    so say the sages
      who preach the religion of Love.

More difficult is welcoming
    dark visitors of loss,
    disappointment, or despair.

To feel abandoned in a universe
    of carelessness or betrayal
    is not the stuff of happy thoughts.

Yet well-seasoned devotees of
    the heart's pure way
    are generously hospitable
    to life's most challenging guests.

Such practice is born of mature experience;
    acceptance is not an early lesson.

Those who persevere through
    earthquake, fire, or raging waters
    come to know that a grateful heart
    transmutes the final dregs of burdens
    once thought vanquished.

Ingratitude in those less mindful lingers—
    hard as the bedrock of resistance,
    the boulder across the road to soul freedom,
    the ball and chain fastened to liberty's ankle.

Uncovering its schemes takes excavation,
    for thanklessness hides in secret caverns,
    emerging in disguise as melancholy,
    or boredom—even sharp analysis
    from bright minds.

But anger lurks in its deepest core—
    erupting when the road gets rough,
    which it will, of course,
    for those most loved by Divinity herself—
    and for whom she goes a-digging
    to wash the diamonds clean at last.

Her clearance may come as a bitter elixir
    that tastes at first of hard surrender,
    but melts to sweetness in the belly
    as the honey of gratitude's gentle tonic
    served up with its warm embrace.

Breaking Through

If resistance could voice its innate defiance,
what would such personified obstinacy say?
   Unaccustomed to being revealed,
      resistance would at first be mute,
      preferring to act, not orate.

   When contrariness is pressed, however,
      it soon responds with noises—
         grunts, groans, moans,
         whimpering n-o-o-o-o-s!
         that sooner or later erupt as...
            I won't. I can't. Don't make me.
            You don't understand.
            I'm afraid.

So, intransigence unwittingly unmasks itself;
exposing resistance as concrete fear—
         the crippler of dreams and hopes
         that builds up walls
         against the very thing
         the soul wants most:
            love, connection, contact,
            presence, comfort, clarity,
            acceptance, receptivity.

Breakthroughs come from embracing defenses.
Not even the most impregnable citadel is truly solid.
Love's sweet breath has a way of detecting fissures.

Letting a Hard Day Be

She was sad today.
And I understood the feeling so well—
    how, like another character
    in the drama of her life,
    the rain-darkened clouds mirrored and amplified
    the terrible shadow sitting on her heart.

Grief's heavy days can arrive just so—
    in a dank cloak that hangs
    about the shoulders like a shroud,
    so cold and lonely you cannot imagine
    ever being happy again.

She didn't want to disappoint the plans we'd made,
But I didn't mind.
    Rainy days are different for me now—
    a welcome retreat for gentle introspection;
    yet I remember well the desperate need to weep.

I didn't try to cheer her up—
    suggesting rather that difficult days
    are often best allowed to fulfill their troubles
    and deserving of respect for the gifts they hold—
    if only of acceptance that comes from
    letting a hard day be itself.

If I were such a day,
    that's how I would want to be honored—
    for the secret wisdom I could offer,
    but only through a quiet space of time and tears.

The Lament

The middle of nowhere is not beautiful.

Dank, dark as wet limestone,
    treacherous in its secrets,
Ready to swallow all your
    hopes and dreams
    in a moment of
    smug inattention
The millisecond before the
    ground you knew,
    or thought you did,
    gives way with sudden power.

Fall down!

Deeper than you knew you could
    onto nothing solid—
    net-less, suspended
    over black water
At the absolute end
    of everything you've been
    till now.

Strip-mined—
That's how loss feels
    sitting in the wound
    that's seared upon your face,
Looking out to the world
    with a bleak eye
    and an empty heart.

A wound that can last
    a lifetime
    or an hour.

Don't try to heal it too soon.

Let it gape out into the open air—
A gash upon your landscape
    that can be
        the opening to a new world
        that only wizards know.

And then only heart
    to heart
    to heart.

What Wizards Know

When the time comes
    that I can look back,

It will seem as fast
    as a lightning flash—

A cosmic interval
    that holds Eternity
    in its gentle grasp.

But here in time
    I miss you.

Will I ever not miss you?

Will nighttime ever feel so full
    that your not being here
    is natural?

> *Breathe, my darling,*
> *I am as close as*
> *your heartbeat.*

Puzzling

there are so many pieces
to fit into this single frame

you have to start with borders
or else there is only chaos

old patterns die hard
and new images emerge only
with relaxed concentration

working on this new puzzle
is the most difficult yet

will deep breathing put
everything in its right place?

the unknown is simply too big
to unscramble without a map

become the map yourself, they say,
as another piece finds its home

Paso Doblé—Spirals in the Dark

It's safe in here, she says to herself.
    The door is locked, the windows barred,
        no way for the creature
        to gain entrance
        to my sanctuary.

Lotus-posed, she seals her peace
        with chant and charm—
        impervious at last.
Ears stopped, shields up,
        lest the howling without
        jar her careful quiet.

But what knock has howl become?
What pounding now
        that her studied protection
        will not drown?

Be still! she shouts.
    You are not welcome in my den.
    Have you no respect for sorrow?
    A minute's peace is all I ask.
    Why won't you go away?

A breath, a beat, a space, a pause—
And then a curdling cry
        that shakes her house
        to its foundation.

Too much! too much! she bleats.
    You've pushed me far enough!

Irate, door flung open, windows ajar,
        eyes wide, ears perked,
        looking out, surprised—
        at nothing after all.

Carefully she closes the door.
Latches, locks, and shutters the portal
        in satisfied relief.

Then turns with sudden shock
        into the face of two fierce eyes
        glowing gold
        above the snarling snout
        that threatens to devour her.

Circling 'round each other now,
        never breaking eye contact,
        they move first left, then right
        in ever-tightening spirals.

Closer and closer
        until he rises up
        and snatches her to his breast;
        not into his glistening maw,
        but to his heart in wild embrace.

And to her great astonishment—
        they dance.

Grace

I cannot be taken
        but I can be received.

I am freely yours
        when you are most in need—
        though you can neither long
        nor pray for me—
        as that which is most
        vehemently sought
        moves ever further away.

Mine is the pathless path
        known by the ancients
        who left maps written
        in star dust—
        visible only to pilgrims used
        to finding their way in the dark.

These are the wanderers
        who expect nothing
        yet receive all—
        who risk all in faith to
        arrive at the threshold
        of my banquet hall
        cloaked only in gratitude
        and smiles.

Mother's Day

I was not a mother, but I was born to one.
Ours was a complicated relationship
    made hard by one's longing
    and the other's resistance
    to too much intimacy.

Consider the alpha mare and embrace her.
Let the clouds part and the rains come
    at last to relax the stress
    of human love's confusion.

There is joy on earth
    in loving acceptance of what is.
I came for her this time and she for me—
    how astonishing to be here
    because a woman gave you life.

A mother does the best she knows,
    and childless daughters
    do not understand the burden.

In Her Shoes

Today I am trying to walk
      in her shoes—a Depression Era baby,
      number five of eight,
      the sensitive one who cried easily
      and longed to be number one of one.

I learned to want what she wanted,
      and mostly kept her happy
      until I turned full on to Spirit's calling
      and broke her heart.
           Years later she broke mine
           by refusing to be me,
           just as I had refused to be her;
           so we both suffered.

I was angry as she lay dying
      because I couldn't stop her pain;
      so I left her in the care of others
      who said I did a beautiful job,
           but I knew I didn't,
           because I couldn't bear
           her anguish
           or mine—
           the hurt we caused each other.

So only today, amidst tears
      of insight and remembrance,
      can I finally feel the love we shared,

and forgive us both—
for failing to be each other;
    and for ultimately succeeding
    in walking in the only shoes
    we could (our own)
    on the path where we were
    both right and both wrong.

The only way it could be
    for this mother and this daughter.

Making My Own Tracks

How does one follow
    in adventurers' tracks
    and reinvent the life
    one has been living?

Another man died yesterday,
    leaving only *I love you*
    in the wake of his departure.

If I were to expire tomorrow,
    what would be the legacy
    of the life I have created?

What is that life?
What is my service to humanity?
What if I were to forsake
    convention and disappear
    into the desert—
    if even for a little while?

A breakthrough is needed—
    a radical embarkation
    into what Sufis call
    a death before death,
        just to practice making
        new tracks in the sand.

A Vision of Passages

You're coming back, aren't you?
But to another, not to me.

The realization hit me
Like a thunderbolt.
Of course, you would do
The radical thing—for Love.

Another letting go of us,
Of dreams that have you waiting,
Serene in ethereal glory,
Till I would make my exit.

But now our work is more apart
Than side by side—or so it seems.
And you long ago made promises
That only you can keep.

You once told me of your visions
For her future life.
She will no doubt have her own.
Mine will come as shocks
To liberate my soul for good.

My task is now to take the plunge
And pass you in the doorway
Once again, my love.

Thoughts at Midnight

Obstacles are dropping away.

What seemed impossible flows
in the light of day.

Commitment counts for all.

Action matters.

Breaking free of timidity
and multiple resistances,
every crutch eventually falls.

No room for mediocrity
or half-way tries.

The way lies clear
in the footprints of faith.

Look for the beacon
in the lighthouse
and you will not falter in the dark.

This was only a test—
fear not.

Dawn's Song

You cannot force the soul to sing
Or produce sonnets on demand
Or offer nosegays of fresh verse
When keeping promises
Is the task at hand.

Some souls can write about their woes
But others find it too much pain
When penetration of their past
Is all that hopes to bring them gain

From consequences good and ill
Of sowings with their companions—
Some recent and some very far
Across the mottled sweep of time.

Yet when the soul feels her heart free
From toil and strife amidst the ruins,
She will raise up songs of joy
And wake you at the dawn with poems.

Past as Prologue

Here I sit midst the fragments of my history—
    trunks of clothes,
    crates of mementos,
    stacks of journals, files,
    papers, reflections,
    ladders of learning,
    ropes for the climb.

While considering their uselessness,
a wiser voice than mine emerged:

    I AM now the scaffolding.

    I hold you in my embrace
        and boost you up the ladder.

    Mine are the seven-league boots—
        my robe the only garment
        you will need for warmth,
        protection, and for comfort.

    Only Love builds lasting stair steps;
        all else is grace—
        and a firmly clasped helping hand
        from the One still truly here.

Quantum Leaping

Forgetting everything I knew,
Burning bridges to the past,
Putting my hand in His or Hers
Or Theirs—for they are
Many and all One.

Futures emerge from what was,
But leaping defies increments.
Only hearts are capable
Of flying to the sun,
Abandoning the structures
That once made them strong.

And no one packs a bag for heaven.

An Open Vessel

What would happen if I opened my heart,
    my entire being, to the deepest
    communion with my beloved?

What would unfold if I allowed myself
    to be guided from the Otherworld
    over the cord that binds us?

What if the future lies not in separation,
    but in union—
    in the connection I have feared
    to believe in or to welcome?

What if destiny portends the combined effort
    of two as one—as a unified heart that
    bridges worlds every moment?

What if I become the open vessel
    into which love's poetry could pour?

For poetry is what calls me.

It was our most sublime connection—
    the language of love we shared
    as metaphor and pure moment.

Part of me wants to succeed alone—
    to prove myself to myself;
    a strange resistance to help,
    a selfish response to love's gift.

So there is the truth of stubbornness
        and refusal to submit,
        even to love from one
        who loves me most.

If I give myself that fully, what will I lose next?
        Will he abandon me again?
        Will I become more nothing?
        Will I shatter like the pot I broke?

        To open completely to love
        is to lose control
        of the illusion of control.

        Liberation occurs when the poet
        becomes the poem
        and allows her self
        to be poured out upon the page.

Destiny Proclaims

*Each new passage
is a walk into darkness.
Opportunity beckons again,
but you can only hear her knock
at a threshold you've already crossed.*

Thoughts Upon Embarking

One hopes—

To be guided
   by the walk itself

To be walked
   by the path

To be spirited
   by the air
   and the sea
   and the mist
   that shrouds you
   from the others

So that each
   may walk alone
   surrounded
   by the true companions
   of one's heart:

The loved
   the lost
   the not yet found
   and most of all
   the Presence of
   the One that touches
   all that is.

Finding Gold in the Interval

The end of life as I've known it—
    standing eagerly at the threshold,
    sensing not to jump too soon
    into what's next.

Till then there's time for excavations—
    some personal archaeology,
    digging into history for clues
    of what may come.

Stories abound in the artifacts
    with many a tear shed
    over adventures past,
    loves lost, victories won.

But signposts are scarce—
    and as the hours crawl by,
    the landscape widens,
    the threshold all but vanishes.

Vast fields appear, ready for harvest,
    gold in the sun, beckoning the scythe,
    summoning my attention
    away from the margin.

Too soon, too soon, the ravens call—
    there's labor in the day
    before your crossing,
    and cycles to complete
    before you sleep in a new bed.

The curtain is falling on the life you knew—
       but the next role is still in casting;
       breathe deep and let your heart
       expand into the interval.

This is a new part with different lines,
       that will have you
        dancing to a novel tune
       you cannot have practiced.

Rushing up to edges is not wise—
       put away your traveling clothes
       and finishing reaping.

Harvests come in many shapes,
       and winter wheat gets planted
       when the field is fallow.

Focus on your native soil—
       not thresholds
       in the distance.

Intimations of the Future

Something is stirring—

    a sensation

    not a thought or feeling
    but a new way of being

    neither proud
    nor ashamed
    of being proud

    honest in presence
    grounded in body

    confident in its expression
    which is rising
    to the surface

    where passion
    can be spoken.

The tree of life
    bears fruit
    that ripens
    with determination,

    but only when left alone.

Unpredictable

Events make clear Eternity's plan
    by happening or not,
    as they so choose.

Wishing the future here
    does not its appearance assure,
    and fortune tellers' minds
    see only what can be foretold,
    but not free will's exactness.

For humans are fickle,
    the present fluid,
    and stars imperfect heralds
    of manifestation.

A good night's sleep is rest indeed
    and medicine for the anxious
    to trust in Spirit and simple prayer
    that all will be revealed in time—

For our highest good is divinely known
    and compassionately wished for.

The Shift

Change seldom comes soon enough
    or else too soon.
        We are so often ahead
        or behind our destiny—
        or what we wish it to be.

Coming attractions can occupy a lot of space
    in the waiting room of life,
    where anticipation masquerades
    as real experience
    and days end up half lived.

Surely, we envision, affairs will turn
    and quickly bring adventure
    back around.

But a wiser universe responds:
    The wheel revolves at its own speed;
        there is nothing you can do,
        so please—
        don't spoil tomorrow's sunrise
        by painting it today.

    Events are shaped by forces larger
        than movie trailers,
        melancholy memories,
        or imagination running off
        before its time.

Transitions need a build-up—
    a gathering of nature's force
    that opens out as roses do
    when buds are left alone to bloom.

Detecting an imminent shift is useful,
    but life can not release the brake
    until your foot comes off the gas.

Navigating the Doldrums

It's easy to miss
    the little bit that happens
    when things won't change—

The imperceptible flutter
    of a butterfly's wing
    that is the fraction
    that's moving
    when things won't change.

Life is not all dust and stasis,
    even when events feel stuck.

Only Love's eye
    detects a breeze
    as soft as baby's breath
    blowing you along.

Sometimes to move forward
    you have to go back
    and pick up what or whom
    you forgot to love—

Or fall in love
    all over again,
    remembering
    what first drew you
    to this place or to that one.

We love for many reasons.

Finding out why again
    may be the particle
    that's moving
    when things don't appear
    to change.

Attunement

Wise heart
    calmly shining,
    centered in
    generous grace.

The Zen point
    of contact
    with all that
    is real and holy.

This is home,
    contented place
    for souls
    to heal.

Wise heart
    radiates and knows
    that timing
    is everything.

Only hallowed space
    can receive
    the prompting
    to move or stay.

Attunement works
    its alchemy
    of change
    right here.

The Catalyst

She was a born change-maker.

Though she meant no harm,
situations and people made major shifts
when she came on the scene;
> and by the time she had moved on,
> no circumstance remained untouched,
>> not even the condition
>> of her own heart.

For life sent her into strange events
that puzzled her for many years,
> until she came to see the pattern
> of enthusiastic beginnings,
> her being filled with pluck and hope
> for what could be accomplished,
>> only to be met with anger,
>> stone walls, and rejection
>> from those she'd come to help.

In early days an innocence
had encouraged her to sally forth;
> but now when a deeper nature beckoned
> that she should seize a perilous cup,
>> her mind recalled in vivid scenes
>> the enigma of her lonely path,
>> in reluctant recollection
>> of the burden she would bear.

For even though she welcomed change
as life's essential principle,
        most folks did not—and blamed her
        for the consequence of their own deeds
            that her presence
            had simply brought to light.

She felt self-doubt impeding her path,
and so questioned her ancient mentors.

But these masterful ones,
        from their wiser view,
        had never found her behavior strange;
        they cherished her disruptions.

And counted as grace her propensity
        to ignite the fresh enlivening flame
        that rouses those who nap so deep
        they do not care to dream.

For wise ones know from ages past
        that till sleepers finally reconnect
        with their own great master plan,
        there can be no magic in their days
        nor lasting sparkle in their nights.

Someone must summon the winds of change
        to rearrange complacency
        and turn inertia to soulful action
        filled with conscious longing.

And the sages always meant, of course,
    for that someone to be her.

So now, when Fortune calls her name,
the catalyst may sigh aloud
in profoundest human reluctance;
        but she, nevertheless, accepts the task
        to wrestle with the enmity
        of those who in their secret hearts
            yearn to shake off
            the hypnotic trance
            imposed on them
            by a drowsy world
                that fears the soul
                on fire for life.

She lives to learn and love and teach,
    to see the once-dull animate,
    to feel the sudden surge of the few
        who catch the wave
        of her inspiration.

And then she knows her passion's reward,
    as they claim the birthright that is theirs,
    turn back to bid her a grateful farewell,
        and disappear
            bright-eyed for good
                over the horizon
                of their destiny.

What If?

What if I acted like a troubadour
    and walked out each day
    into the world around me
    to experience it with joy
    and curiosity for life
    as an adventure in full color—
        fully embodied,
        inhabited from the inside
        as my own true living
        of the dreams
        I have dared not allow
        myself to know?

What if I relished the morrow
    as an opportunity to write
    and paint landscapes
    to show my deep appreciation
    for being on this earth—
        to capture
        just a handful of stardust
        in order to share
        a touch of radiance
        with hearts who need
        a bit of sunshine?

What if I were to throw off
    the shackles of mistaken identity
    and claim my birthright
    as a free spirit,

as one who is unencumbered
by the opinions of others
or the shame
of being pushed and pulled
in directions
they would have me go?

What if all that has gone before
truly is prologue
and I am today
liberated,
to go forth,
banners flying,
to write my own destiny,
to contribute
a joyful presence,
and to feel worthy
of this life
that is my own—
not according
to anyone's plan
but Spirit's—
the one we agreed upon
so very long ago?

What if has turned
into why not—
and I can't think of
a single reason.

At Day's End

a day of destiny—
and of turning
toward the Light

hand in hand
beside each other

to face the Sun as one

and sing its praises
with harmonious tones

in a singular chord

whose resonance
can change the world

A Glimmering Sense of Purpose

To embark upon the inner journey
   is to open a door
   frequented by dreamers.

Spirit is eager for your company
   and rushes in
   to carry you aloft
   on this new adventure
   whose fulfillment
   waits upon your will.

The soul knows
   what she's doing
   and gladly packs her bags.

Your ancient calling beckons—
   the voyage has begun.

Acknowledgements

I have heard it said that gratitude opens the way to all other blessings. Life has proved to me the truth of that statement many times over.

I know of several people who create gratitude journals as a practice that keeps them in that attitude—to maintain the open heart and mind that gratitude nurtures.

For me, writing poetry has the same effect of opening my heart and mind to a flow of enlightening experience.

The poetical atmosphere is a mystical space, a realm of consciousness to which I find myself homing. The opportunity to visit that place and live there for periods of time is a grace for which I am eternally grateful.

The muse is a marvelous aspect of being. I do not pretend to fully understand her or him. Inspiration appears in a number of guises. And isn't that part of the beautiful mystery that has for centuries beckoned poets to brave the Unknown in hopes of coming out the other side with a few lines that may delight or inspire or even heal.

Such is my experience and a profound reason for the gratitude I am offering here along with profound thanks to my colleagues Theresa McNicholas, James Bennett, and Paula Kehoe, and to the artists whose public domain images we have chosen for this volume.

May you, dear reader, feel my gratitude flow from these verses. Writing them has been a gift that I am joyfully grateful to share.

A Poet of Soul & Fire

Cheryl Lafferty Eckl is a mystical poetess and storyteller who writes in the ecstatic tradition of Rumi and Hafiz.

She lives in Livingston, Montana, where she finds profound inspiration in the surrounding mountains, rivers, lakes, and Big Sky spaces that have long been recognized as places of spiritual connection and healing.

An award-winning author of multiple books, Cheryl continues to embrace life's myriad transitions as she writes, teaches, and pays deep attention to the poetics of her soul.

To learn more about her work, please visit her website at www.CherylEckl.com.

www.ingramcontent.com/pod-product-compliance
Lightning Source LLC
Chambersburg PA
CBHW020658300426
44112CB00007B/426